THE STORY OF
HANUKKAH

THE STORY OF HANUKKAH

by DAVID A. ADLER

illustrated by Jill Weber

Holiday House / New York

Happy Hanukkah to Jacob and Yoni
and their parents, Michael and Deborah—D. A. A.
For Sterling and Rainer—J. W.

The menorah in the Temple during the Maccabees' time had seven branches,
but today's Hanukkah menorahs hold nine candles, one for each of the eight
nights of the holiday and the Shamash, the candle used to light the others.

Text copyright © 2011 by David A. Adler
Illustrations copyright © 2011 by Jill Weber
All Rights Reserved
HOLIDAY HOUSE is registered in the U.S. Patent and Trademark Office.
Printed and bound in July 2020 at Tien Wah Press, Johor Bahru, Johor, Malaysia.
The text typeface is Celestia Antiqua.
The artwork was painted in acrylics.
11 13 15 17 19 20 18 16 14 12

Library of Congress Cataloging-in-Publication Data
Adler, David A.
The Hanukkah story / by David A. Adler ; illustrated by Jill Weber. — 1st ed.
p. cm.
ISBN 978-0-8234-2295-1 (hardcover)
1. Hanukkah—Juvenile literature.
I. Weber, Jill. II. Title.
BM695.H3A6515 2011
296.4'35—dc22
2010029879

ISBN 978-0-8234-2457-1
(paperback)

The Hanukkah story begins in Israel a long time ago, when it was called Judea. At that time the Jews who lived there were farmers and shepherds.

On holidays they all went to the beautiful Temple in Jerusalem. The Temple was on top of a mountain and called the House of God. Its gates were covered with gold and silver. Inside was a *ner tamid*, a light that always burned.

For a long time the Jews lived in peace,
although they did not rule their land.

Then a Greek, Antiochus IV, became king.

He tore down the walls of Jerusalem. Thousands were
killed. Anyone who lit Sabbath candles, studied Jewish law,
or refused to bow to Greek idols was put to death.

The king's men came to the town of Modiin. They demanded that Mattathias, an old priest, worship one of their gods.

Mattathias refused. He threw down the idol and called out, "Whoever is for the Lord, our God, follow me!"

Mattathias ran to the hills.
His five sons and many other
Jews followed him.

Antiochus's army chased after Mattathias. But when the soldiers came near, brave Jews hiding behind large rocks and inside caves attacked. Then they ran back to the hills and hid.

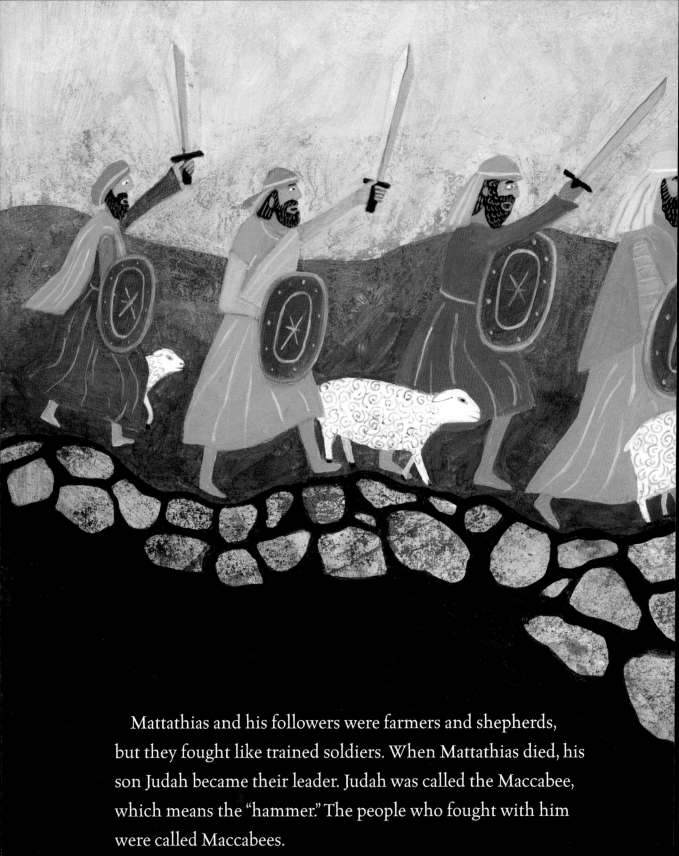

Mattathias and his followers were farmers and shepherds, but they fought like trained soldiers. When Mattathias died, his son Judah became their leader. Judah was called the Maccabee, which means the "hammer." The people who fought with him were called Maccabees.

The king's armies came with bows, arrows, swords, horses, and armored elephants; but they weren't able to beat the Maccabees.

In the final battle, there were
more than six armed soldiers to each
Maccabee, but still the mighty army
of Antiochus was beaten.

Judah then led the Maccabees to Jerusalem.

The Maccabees cried when they saw the Temple ruined and filled with garbage. They cleaned it.

They built a new altar, new gates, and new doors.

When it came time to light the *ner tamid*, they found
just one small jar of pure oil, only enough to burn for one
day. But that oil burned for eight days—until more oil could
be prepared.

On the twenty-fifth day of the Hebrew month of Kislev, the Temple again became the "House of God."

Judah declared that every year on that date an eight-day holiday would begin. The holiday was called Hanukkah, which means "dedication." It celebrates the day the Temple was rededicated.

That was more than two thousand years ago.

Today, all over the world, Jews celebrate Hanukkah by lighting
candles, singing Hanukkah songs, and eating latkes—potato pancakes—
and *sufganiyot*—jelly doughnuts. Latkes and *sufganiyot* are prepared in oil
and remind Jews of the Hanukkah miracles.

In many homes people exchange Hanukkah gifts.

Children also play a game with a four-sided spinning top called a
dreidel. On each side of the dreidel is a different Hebrew letter, the first
letters of the Hebrew sentence *Nes gadol hayah sham*, which means "A
great miracle happened there." It happened in Jerusalem.

Hanukkah celebrates one of the first fights for religious freedom.

Jill Weber's recipe for

LATKES

This recipe makes about 20 latkes.

An adult to help

A potato peeler

A large bowl

A grater

A colander

An eggbeater or
  electric mixer

A frying pan

A spatula

Paper towels

2 pounds of white potatoes, the
  older the better (about 6 or 7)

1 onion, peeled

2 eggs, separated into yolks and
  whites

3 tablespoons matzo meal or flour

salt and pepper to taste

1/2 cup canola oil for the pan

1. Peel the potatoes and put in a bowl of cold water until ready to use.

2. Using the largest opening on the grater, grate the potatoes and the onion. The onion will help keep the potatoes from turning brown.

3. Squeeze as much as possible of the liquid out of the grated potato and onion mixture over the bowl.

4. Place the grated mixture in a colander draining over the bowl. After a couple of minutes, the liquid will have separated, leaving a starchy paste at the bottom of the bowl. Discard the liquid but keep the starch.

5. Add the potato and onion mixture, egg yolks, matzo meal, salt, and pepper to the potato starch. Mix thoroughly.

6. Beat the eggs whites to shiny, stiff peaks. Fold them into the potato mixture.

7. With an adult helping you, pour about 1/4 inch of oil in the pan. Heat the oil in the pan until it is very hot. Drop tablespoonfuls of the potato mixture into the pan.

8. Turn the latkes only once until both sides are very brown and the potatoes are cooked through.

9. Place on paper towels to drain while
   you fry the next batch.

Serve with applesauce or sour cream.

*(It was my job to grate the potatoes and the onion when I was a little
girl. My hands smelled like onion for what seemed like a week.)*

HOW to PLAY DREIDEL

Each player begins with an equal number of pieces of Hanukkah gelt, raisins, nuts, pennies, or other small tokens.

Everyone puts one token in the pot.

Each player spins the dreidel and then adds, subtracts, or does nothing to the pot depending on how the dreidel falls.

Nun stands for *nisht*, or "nothing," so the player doesn't do anything.

Gimel stands for *gantz*, or "everything," so the player gets the whole pot.

Heth stands for *halb*, or "half," so the player gets half of the pot. (If there is an odd number of tokens, the player takes half of the pot plus one.)

Shin means *shtel*, or "put in," so the player adds a token to the pot.

Whenever the pot is empty, everyone adds one token to make a new pot.

A player who runs out of tokens is out of the game.

The game is over when one player has won everything.